You Are Remarkably and Wonderfully Made

AVEREY N. A. BRYAN

To order additional copies of this book, contact:
Xlibris
844-714-8691
www.Xlibris.com
Orders@Xlibris.com

Library of Congress Control Number: 2023911772
ISBN: Softcover   979-8-3694-0192-7
       Hardcover   979-8-3694-0194-1
       EBook   979-8-3694-0193-4

Print information available on the last page

Rev. date: 06/26/2023

This book was written to help you understand that though you may not have the same beliefs or experiences as others, or even me, we can learn from each other. We were all created by God, and he has some amazing things to say about us. On the following pages, you will get a glimpse of who you truly are rather than what society or others say about you.

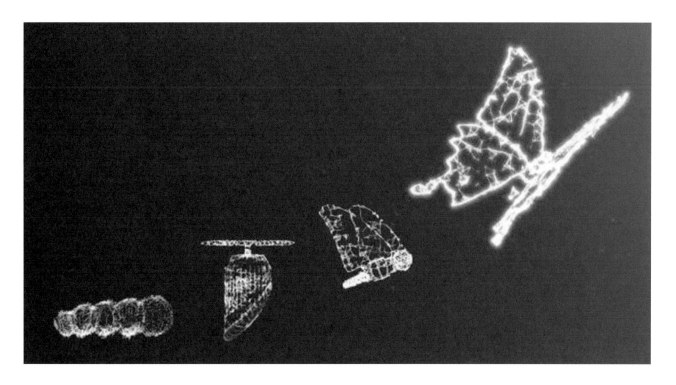

I will praise you because I am remarkably and wonderfully made.
Your works are wonderful and I know this very well.

—Psalm 139:14

This Bible verse may not be one that you believe just yet, but I promise you that if you recite it daily, it will sink into your soul and you *will* start believing it. I didn't believe that I was remarkably and wonderfully made growing up, for many reasons. I didn't grow up with my parents so I often felt incomplete.

Today, you too might be feeling "incomplete," but I am here to tell you that you matter; you are complete and beautiful in every way. You were meant to be here and deserve all the good things life has to offer. You got this!

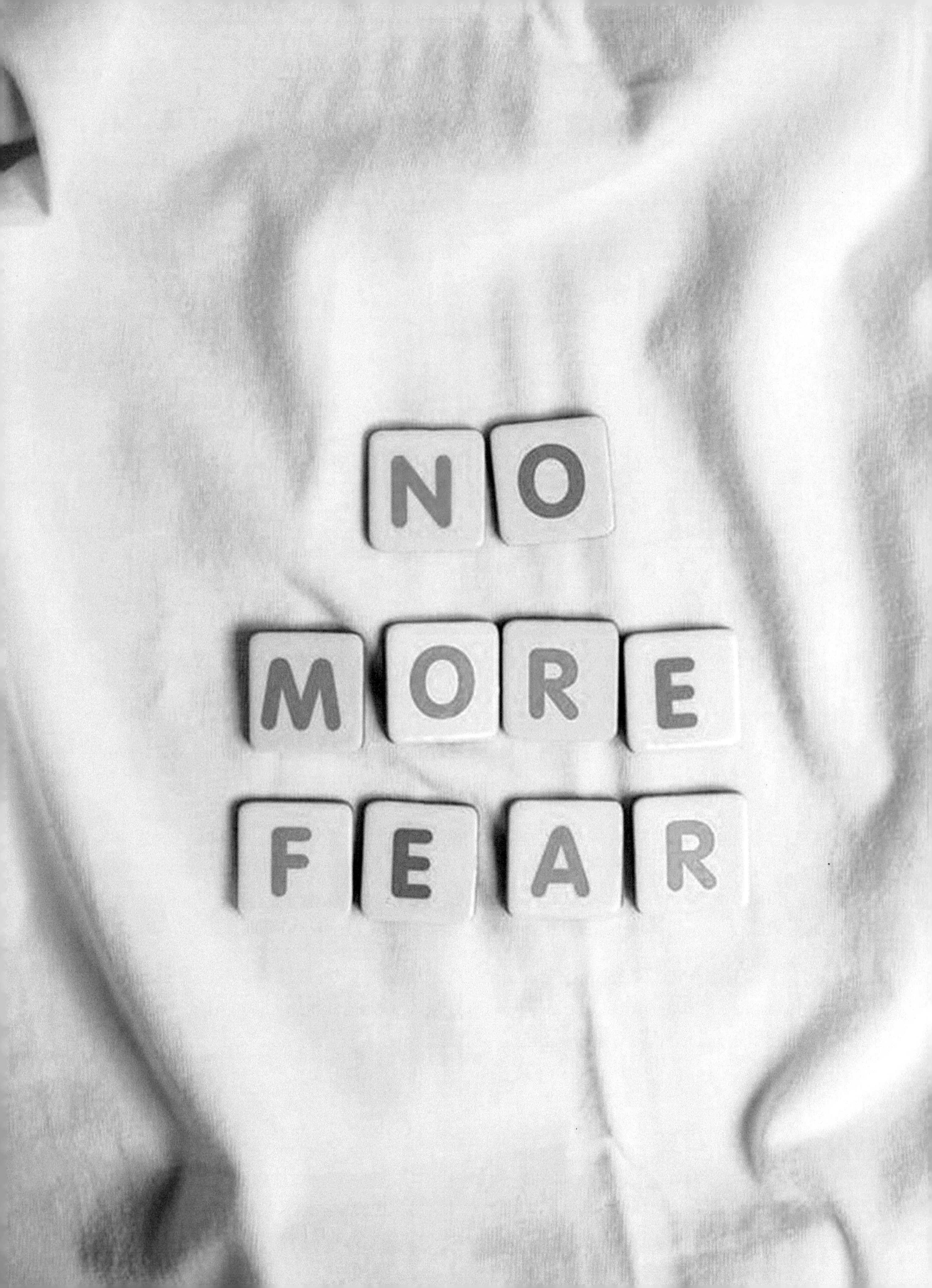
NO
MORE
FEAR

Fear: What is fear?

Fear is an unpleasant emotion that is caused by the belief that someone or something dangerous can cause pain or is a threat *(The Oxford Dictionary).*

For God has not given us a spirit of fear and timidity, but of power, love, and a sound mind (2 Timothy 1:7).

Many times you get fearful. You are afraid that you don't fit in, you are afraid of making mistakes, and you are afraid of being a failure. You are afraid to disappoint people you care about, and you are afraid of being hurt by people or things. When you believe in God, you do not have to be afraid because his Holy Spirit that lives inside you will give you the power to overcome all your fears. Easier said than done, huh? I know. I have struggled and still struggle with fear, but it strengthens me to know that I can constantly remind myself of God's assurance that the spirit of fear does not have to take me over because it is not a part of who he is.

At your age, it is completely normal to be fearful. Every one of you has your own experiences, some more scary than others, but there is always someone who has had the same experiences as you. You are not alone! Continue to dream big, even through the fear. When Malala Yousafzai decided to fight for the rights of girls to be educated in her country, she was fearful but did not allow it to stop her from fighting for what she believed in. Though she was critically hurt, she went on to gain a Nobel Peace Prize as her voice was heard all over the world.

Another verse that helps me through my fear is Deuteronomy 31:6. "Be strong and courageous. Do not be afraid or terrified because of them, for the Lord YOUR God goes with you; he will never leave you nor forsake you." He is *your* God, and he will help you conquer that fear. These seeds that the devil planted do not have to become a tree that overshadows your life. They will be stifled out by the spirit of God. You do not have to water those seeds. Let them starve, and eventually they will die.

Shame

Oftentimes along with fear there is shame. Maybe you did something that no one knows about or had something happen to you that you feel like you cannot share so you have not shared it because you are ashamed.

What is shame?

Shame is "a painful feeling of humiliation or distress caused by a regrettable situation or action" *(The Oxford Dictionary).*

The Bible has many stories of people who have done things that have caused them to feel shame; however, it also tells of Jesus's love and mercy toward them. He smiled at them, he allowed them to touch him, he sat and ate with them, and he spoke up on their behalf. The tax collector Zacchaeus, who was a thief, invited him to dinner and he went to his house to eat with him, even though he knew he was a thief (Luke 19:1–10). He stood up for the woman who was being stoned because she was dating another woman's husband (John 8:1–11). Both persons did something shameful and were expected to be ashamed, but what if you didn't cause your shame?

Sometimes people violate us and cause us to feel ashamed for something we did not have any control over and somehow make us feel like we did something wrong in the process. Can I tell you something? This is a big, fat *lie!* This was *not* your fault! Repeat after me. "That was not my fault. That was not my fault. That was not my fault. I do not have to be ashamed of someone else's actions toward me." Take a moment and let that sink in.

OK, breathe. That feels a little better, doesn't it?

Now think of how Jesus wants you to feel. He wants you to know that he does not see you as shameful. He sees you as his child whom he loves. He sees you as someone whom he will sit down and eat a burrito with, a salad with, a bacon egg and cheese on a bagel sandwich with. How 'bout that ice cream? Ummm. Yah, that too. He loves you so much and sees that special person that is *you!*

Just in case you did something that you are ashamed of (e.g., you stole that money from your mom's purse or cheated on that test), you can admit your guilt to God and he will forgive you. John 1:9 says God is faithful and reliable. If we confess our sins, he forgives them and cleanses us from *everything* we've done wrong.

When someone has caused you to feel shame for something that is not your fault to begin with (e.g., if you were abused by a family member, friend, or someone you trust), know that this is a lie from the devil.

You do not need to be ashamed because you did nothing wrong. You are not responsible for someone else's actions against you. God's word tells you in Isaiah 50:7–8a (GNT), But their insults cannot hurt me because the Sovereign Lord gives me help, I brace myself to endure them. I know that I will not be disgraced for God is near and he will prove me innocent.

Guilt: Feeling responsible or regretful for a perceived offense, real or imaginary *(The Oxford Dictionary)*.

Guilt usually accompanies shame; they go hand in hand. You can feel guilty about something then it causes shame, or feel ashamed and it causes guilt. Either way, you do not have to live there. "So now there is no condemnation for those who are in Christ Jesus" (Romans 8:1). What this means is that you do not have to live with guilt even if you've done something wrong but especially when you have been wronged. When you draw near to God, he will remove that guilt and replace it with freedom, joy, love, and peace.

It is hard to forgive someone who has done something to make us fearful, guilty, ashamed, or unworthy. You now have become resentful and bitter toward them. The weird thing is that these feelings may be projected onto others who have in no way hurt us. These include our family members, friends, and people we truly care about. When we hurt those we love because we are hurting, we can become withdrawn, sometimes due to guilt and shame for our actions, fear of letting them know what is wrong, or because of buried emotions. It becomes a cycle of pain. You may be able to relate to what I am saying. Stop for a moment and think of how you have acted toward someone who did not hurt you but because you were triggered by an action, something that was said, or by a thought that ran across your own mind. You hurt their feelings. How can you make that right? Guess what. You must never just sweep those reactions under the rug. Always acknowledge that you acted in a way that was unkind and offer a sincere apology. This might be hard at first, so if you cannot do it face-to-face, try writing them a note. You can explain how their action affected you and apologize for how you reacted. You can also explain that you were just feeling sad about something, if you do not want to share what it is. You do not have to share, if you are not ready. Just let them know how you were feeling at the time. That will help them to understand why you were upset. They might be able to think of ways to avoid those behaviors in the future or how to do or say things differently next time. Compromising also helps to avoid future issues. Sometimes bitterness and resentment can have you thinking bad thoughts about those with whom you are upset, dwelling on the negative things will only cause you more pain. I often hear people say that unforgiveness is like drinking poison and expecting the other person to die. Listen. I know how hard it is to forgive, but I also know that I don't like how unforgiveness makes me feel. It makes my chest tight and it is hard to breathe; my jaws stiff, my face hard and cold. That weight is way too heavy for someone as young as you to walk around with too.

I came across a Bible verse that I have heard so many times but that just jumped out at me one day when I was complaining about someone who had done me wrong and I decided that dwelling on my pain was not where I wanted to be as this was separating me from God. That verse is Philippians 4:8. "Finally, my friends, keep your minds on whatever is true, pure, right, holy, friendly, and proper. Don't ever stop thinking about what is truly worthwhile and worthy of praise" (Contemporary English Version). Now whenever I begin to have bad thoughts, whether about myself or others, I repeat this verse, and you can too! Do not let anyone steal your joy. You are too precious.

Fueled by happy thoughts.

Bitterness: "Anger and disappointment at being treated unfairly; resentment" *(The Oxford Dictionary).*

Bitterness grows as a result of unresolved anger and emotions that you have not dealt with. It is also a reflection that you have not allowed yourself to grieve over actions committed against you and even those that you have committed yourself. It will manifest itself in an inability to control your actions when triggered. Bitterness is evidence that you have not forgiven others and yourself, and this will destroy you if you do not let go of it. So now the question becomes this: how do I get rid of bitterness, and dare I suggest that it might first be do I want to get rid of this bitterness?

If you are feeling bitter toward someone, this causes you to get hot from the inside out when you see, hear, or talk about this person. Your heart races, you feel like you can't breathe, and you get angry. Is this a feeling you want for the rest of your life? Bitterness is causing you to be sick, it is destroying your body and your soul, and it is sucking the life out of you. Newsflash: that person or situation is controlling you! I know that the one thing hurt people like is control. We want to control all the situations we can, so why is it that we are content with those persons or situations controlling us? Let go of that familiar feeling of holding on to bitterness, and it will have to let go of you too. Guess what. You are in control. If you tell bitterness, anger, guilt, shame, fear, and condemnation to get out of your life, they will go! It is these feelings that need you; you do not need them. If you stop watering plants, they will eventually die. Think of these feelings/emotions as plants. They will not continue to grow if they are not watered, pruned, or tended to. Even succulents die, and these need very little water, but guess who kills succulents. Yes, me! I do not have a green thumb. I am the worst farmer, and I want to be the worst farmer of negative feelings and emotions that want to keep me down. These things that depend on me to feed them so that they will kill me slowly—Uhh, no, ma'am. Not me. I'm good. Now your turn. Say it out loud. "I will not water you anymore. You will not control me or kill me. No, ma'am!" Repeat it until you believe it.

Ephesians 4:31–32 (Amplified Bible) says, "Let all bitterness and wrath and anger and clamor (animosity, resentment, strife, fault-finding) and slander be put away from you, along with every kind of malice (all spitefulness, verbal abuse, malevolence). Be kind and helpful to one another, tenderhearted (compassionate, understanding) forgiving one another (readily and freely), just as God in Christ forgave you." These verses tell us what to let go of and what to replace it with. I know it's not easy, but when you want to live, and live as God intended you to live, to fulfill your purpose, it is worth letting go of.

The rest of this book is filled with affirmations to help you get through each day. Choose as many as you wish each morning when you wake up, and repeat them throughout the day. Take each day moment by moment, and know that it is OK to make mistakes. They help you grow and improve.

Loads of love,

Averey.

smart

beautiful

kind

Wah nuh dead nuh call it duppy! If it's not dead, do not call it a ghost.

I am Jamaican, and this is a Jamaican saying. It means that you should never count anyone out because when they're still alive, they have a chance of being great.

I am alive today, and I will accomplish great things.

Make a list of the top five things you want to accomplish today.

- _____

- _____

- _____

- _____

- _____

I am beautiful/handsome inside and out.

I will praise you because I am remarkably and wonderfully made.
Your works are wonderful and I know this very well

(Psalm 139:14)

List five things that make you beautiful/handsome inside and out.

- _____

- _____

- _____

- _____

- _____

I am worthy.

Luke 12:6–7:

Are not five sparrows sold for two pennies? And not one of them is forgotten before God. Why, even the hairs of your head are all numbered. Fear not; you are of more value than many sparrows.

No matter what negative things have been said to you or about in the past, these do not define you. They are not the truth, not your truth. God's words about you are the only words that are true and all that matter.

List five things that make you worthy.

- _____

- _____

- _____

- _____

- _____

I am loved.

Jeremiah 31:3–4:

I have loved you with an everlasting love; therefore, I have continued my faithfulness toward you. Again I will build you and you shall be built.

To infinity and beyond! That is not even as long as everlasting. Everlasting means that something lasts forever. Imagine being loved forever regardless of what you do. That, my friend, is pretty cool to me. It is incomparable because people fall in and out of love constantly. Some people's love is conditional and we get hurt by it, but with God's love, that ain't it. He loves forever!

List five reasons you are worthy of love.

- _____

- _____

- _____

- _____

- _____

I am important.

Isaiah 49:16:

Behold, I have engraved you on the palms of my hands.

I have some tattoos with my kids' names. My daughter in particular wanted me to tattoo just her name by itself on my body. She even suggested the place. This gesture indicates to her how important she is to me, and it makes her feel important, special, loved, and happy. Just as this gesture fills my daughter's heart with joy, having your name engraved on God's palm is high honor. It shows how important you are to him. He has tattooed your name on his palm! Whew, chil'. I don't know about you, but I am excited about this. It makes my heart sing and my soul happy. I hope you can get excited about that with me, because *you* are important!

List five ways in which you are important to yourself or other.

- _____

- _____

- _____

- _____

- _____

I am brave.

Joshua 1:9:

Have I not commanded you? Be strong and courageous. Do not be frightened, and do not be dismayed, for the Lord your God is with you wherever you go.

*G*od not only tells you to be strong and brave, but he also tells you why. He says that he is with you wherever you go. Regardless of where that is, he is with you. You cannot run away from him. Even if you are mad at him, he is with you. I hope you are excited about that, because I am.

List five ways that you can be brave.

- _____

- _____

- _____

- _____

- _____

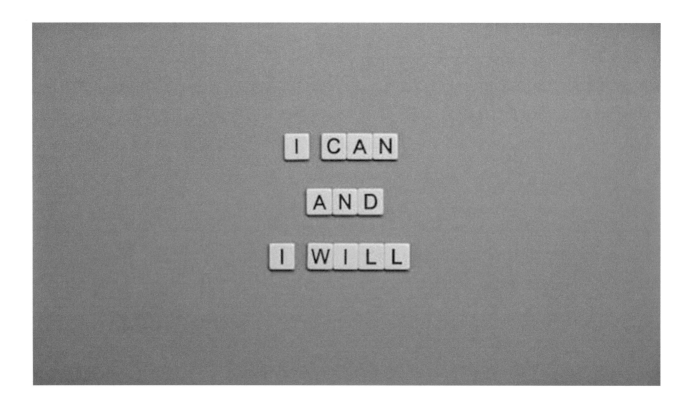

I am capable.

Philippians 4:13:

I can do all things through Christ who gives me strength.

Say what? You can do *all* things. Not some. Not just what people expect you to do or want you to do. You can do what you dream about doing. You can do crazy things, make boss moves, and be great at it. Why? Because God has given you the ability to do it. He gives you the strength to get back up again when you fail, to push through the difficult times, to learn from your mistakes. He gives you the strength to listen to the rejections and come back swinging. God doesn't play with the people he loves; he's *gotchu!*

List five things you are capable of.

- _____

- _____

- _____

- _____

- _____

I am enough.

Ephesians 2:10:

For we are God's handiwork, created in Christ Jesus to do good works, which God prepared in advance for us to do.

I know you like to be in control and so you prepare for things as best as you can, but look at God's level of preparedness! He's next level. He already prepared our path through life even before our parents were born! You were created to do good works. That means that though you may fail, you will do well. When you put God first and never give up, that is also part of the recipe to success.

List five reasons why you are enough.

- _____

- _____

- _____

- _____

- _____

I am perfect just the way I am.

2 Corinthians 12:9:

But he said to me, "My grace is sufficient for you, for my power is made perfect in weakness. Therefore I will boast all the more gladly in my weaknesses, so that the power of Christ may rest upon me."

The apostle Paul was having a hard time but God told him that he does not need to worry about being scared because it is through this fear that he is building him up.

It is through this fear that Paul is drawing closer to God because it is the fear that makes him dependent on God and not dependent on himself. When we depend on ourselves to solve problems, we tend to make ourselves idols. We think that it is through our own efforts that we succeed and forget about the One who had this all planned out from before we were born. Acknowledging that you are imperfect but perfect just the way you are is what Christ desires, and he is with you through it all. He is using this imperfection to tell you that you are indeed perfect just the way you are; you are unique.

List five things that make you *younique.*

- _____

- _____

- _____

- _____

- _____

I am free.

Galatians 1:5:

*It is for freedom that Christ has set us free. Stand firm, then, and
do not let yourselves be burdened again by a yoke of slavery.*

Yass, freedom! Who doesn't like the thought of being free? Free to go out with friends, free to stay up late, and free to do whatever it is that we want to do. Freedom is desired from a young age. When you were a small child, you wanted to feed yourself, pushing away the spoon and turning your face away because you wanted your parents to put it down so you could do it yourself. You wanted to choose your own clothes, etc. You just wanted a sense of authority over your own life. Well, Jesus died so that we may have freedom. The devil put some stumbling blocks in your path. He told you that you'll never be good enough, you'll never be loved, and you cannot achieve this goal. Who is he? He is a liar, a deceiver, and a coward! Jesus set you free when he died on the cross for you. Even if you have been a victim, you are still free. Yes, free to accomplish all your goals and dreams, free to love and be loved, and free to do whatever you want. Though you are free, you have to remember that Jesus still wants you to do good to other and to be careful to keep his commandments.

Galatians 5:13 says, "You, my brothers and sisters, were called to be free. But do not use your freedom to indulge the flesh; rather, serve one another humbly in love."

List five things you are free to do.

- _____

- _____

- _____

- _____

- _____

Feel.

I want to end by encouraging you to *feel.* What do I mean by this? I want you to acknowledge your emotions and allow yourself to experience those emotions that you keep pushing down. Allow yourself to experience the emotions that you keep ignoring. Allow yourself to experience those emotions that you think make you look weak and vulnerable. Know that vulnerability does not make you weak. It humbles you. It builds you up so that you can be stronger than you are now.

When you do not allow yourself to go through the emotions, you are not going to heal. You will continue to walk around in the lies that you were made to believe about yourself. Let me tell you a secret. I had not allowed myself to feel all the hurt that I had buried inside. As a child and adult, I suffered from abuses, and because of that, I could not truly love and allow myself to be loved by anyone. I did not believe that God could love me. It was not until I allowed myself to *feel* that I was able to release these emotions. The release was not a pretty one. It did not feel good because I was so accustomed to not feeling. I had to make a conscientious decision to go through the process because I was tired of the weight of my pain. So I cried and cried and cried some more. I allowed myself to remember my trauma so that I could feel all the emotions and then release them. This is a process, and it is not over. To be honest, it is never over, but it gets easier, the weight gets lighter, and you begin to feel more of your emotions, releasing them as they come rather than holding on to them. Take it from me: it is a beautiful feeling.

As you go through your journey of self-discovery and healing, trust God through the process and give yourself a break. It is OK to make mistakes. It is OK to cry and be vulnerable. It is OK to be angry, sad, happy, or fearful. Best of all, it is OK to love and to be loved because *you are worth it!*

God's Promises to You

I am always with you.

Isaiah 41:10:

Fear not for I am with you; do not be dismayed, for I am your God; I will strengthen you, I will help you, I will uphold you with my righteous right hand.

I will never leave you.

Deuteronomy 31:8:

I will never leave you nor forsake you. Do not be afraid; do not be discouraged.

I will always lift you up.

Psalm 37:23–24:

The Lord makes firm the steps of the one who delights him, though you may stumble, you will not fall, the Lord upholds you with his hand.

I am fighting for you.

Exodus 14:14:

The Lord will fight for you.

I will take care of all your needs.

Philippians 4:19:

And my God will supply every need of yours according to his riches in glory in Christ Jesus.

I will answer your prayers.

Matthew 7:7–8:

"Ask, and it will be given to you; seek and you will find; knock and it will be opened to you. For everyone who asks receives, and the one who knocks it will be opened."

Nothing can separate you from me.

Romans 8:38–39:

"For I am sure that neither death nor life, nor angels nor rulers, nor things Present nor things to come, nor powers, nor height nor depth, nor anything else in all creation, will be able to separate us from the love of God in Christ Jesus our Lord."

I keep my promises.

2 Corinthians 1:20:

"For all of God's promises have been fulfilled in Christ with a resounding "Yes!" And through Christ, our "Amen" ascends to God for his glory."

Averey N. A. Bryan is a woman of God, a mother of three and an educator who enjoys reading and writing poetry. She wrote this book with a desire to empower her daughter to be every bit of what God created her to be and to drown out the negative energies all around. As you read, may your spirit be uplifted and may you experience peace.

Printed in the United States
by Baker & Taylor Publisher Services